The Demons Are Done Dancing

The Demons Are Done Dancing

Danny Mahlon Underwood

authorHOUSE®

AuthorHouse™
1663 Liberty Drive
Bloomington, IN 47403
www.authorhouse.com
Phone: 1-800-839-8640

First published by AuthorHouse   08/30/2011

ISBN: 978-1-4634-0454-3 (sc)
ISBN: 978-1-4634-1278-4 (ebk)

Library of Congress Control Number: 2011908076

Printed in the United States of America

Any people depicted in stock imagery provided by Thinkstock are models, and such images are being used for illustrative purposes only.
Certain stock imagery © Thinkstock.

This book is printed on acid-free paper.

CONTENTS

There is something special about having a place like my 40 acre farm to escape to when your real world gets too noisy. It's a place to see out of the ordinary things and nature in its rawest form. You never know what you will see when you go down there.

My advice is to get out of your element once in awhile. Expand your comfort zone a little. You might actually enjoy the experience.

The format of **'The Demons Are Done Dancing'** is much like a mirror of my life.

It starts out light & carefree with a heart of a child humor, but ends up in a deep darkness. In a place that sometimes even I cannot understand.

Yet it is a place where I finally find peace. A place that I have spent 35 years searching for.

This book is going to be a tough read for a lot of people. I know, because it was tough for me to write.

It completes a collection of poetry that is my life.

This poem is about my legendary eating habits-heavy on the habits. Cheeseburgers and fries almost everyday, chocolate by the handful, raw pie dough and coke.

The Doctor told me to change my habits because of the physical toll it was taking on my body.

So I'm eating less "bad foods" and physically I do feel better, but it has left me with an unenergetic and lethargic mind.

This must be what it is like to live to be 100 years old. Yea, it's a great accomplishment, but what the hell is the point of living that long if you don't enjoy it.

If I survive without the massive heart attack only to live long enough to get cancer, I'm going to be one pissed off individual. Thanks a lot you Quack!

Junk Food Junkie

Coke is my methanphedime;
Chocolate is my cocaine.
Red meat, my marijuania;
I use it everyday.

M & M's are like uppers;
Reese's Peanut Butter cup is my crank.
My body is like a misfiring car;
There is sugar in my tank.

My blood pressure is through the roof;
My cholesterol off the chart.
When they finally cut my chest open;
They'll find nothing but a candy heart.

Just like a Hostess Twinkie;
I'm fluffy and full of cream.
I sit on the throne as King Ding Dong;
Little Debbie is the girl of my dreams.

I eat cookie dough by the bowl;
And pie dough for a midnight snack.
Apple Pie is like a heroin fix;
And cheesecake is my crack.

I'm a junk food junkie;
Right now I need a fix.
Do I feel like a Butterfinger;
Or should I have a Twix?

Bedtime On The Farm

Laying in the bed of my truck;
Serenaded by the oil wells lullaby.
I can see silhouettes in the field;
Of deer grazing in the moonlit night.

I watch them with pure amazement;
As they mosey around this land of mine.
To them it is no big deal;
To me, it's an experience of a lifetime.

Tonight they are free to roam;
Without the threat of harm.
It's incredible the things that go on;
In the middle of the night down on the farm.

Things most folks never witness;
I have been lucky enough to see.
Only because I am crazy enough;
To sleep in the bed of my Chevy.

My wife wouldn't enjoy this;
Not that she wouldn't sleep in the car;
But the hoot owl that is my alarm clock;
Doesn't come equipped with a snooze bar.

We are all fascinated by the deaths of celebrities even though most of them we've never met in person.

In reality, they are just like us. None of them have ever died in a manner any different than other people we have never heard of.

But, sometimes I think they have their own Grim Reaper.

The Idol Taker

You cannot blame the man;
With the wings on his arm.
For losing Buddy's plane;
On that Clear Lake, Iowa farm.

Nor can you fault;
That air-headed twit.
Who fed John Belushi;
His fatal speed-ball hit.

When the Idol Taker grabs a hold of you;
It will not let loose.
It grips you tighter and tighter;
Like a swinging oak tree noose.

It was guiding those bullets;
As Tupac rolled down the strip.
And driving both of the buses;
On Jimmy and Janis' last trips.

It was there the night;
Elvis collapsed to the floor at Graceland.
And pulled hard the trigger;
On the shotgun in Cobain's hand.

When it picks you as its next victim;
You're at the mercy of its will.
The Idol Taker's only talent;
Is it knows how to kill.

A friend of mine, Ron Lybarger once compared this next poem to the style of Charles Bukowski. (Ron is an English teacher at Eisenhower High School in Decatur, Il. He also leads a creative writing class and a Poetry Club, Veritas, which I have spoken to on a couple of occasions.)

I, not being a connoisseur on the subject and will certainly never be heard uttering the phrase, "I'll take Famous Literature for $500, Alex." I had to research Charles Bukowski's work.

I was both pleasantly surprised and flattered at the comparison from someone as versed in the subject as Ron is.

Words From A Bottle

His smoked filled eyes struggle to see
Yellow are they
Like the blank pages before him.

He sips his glass of liquid thoughts
Vodka
His choice of inspiration melts the cubes of ice.

The pulp of his orange juice
Settles to the bottom
He stirs the drink like a gambler pulling on a one-armed bandit.

No jackpot.

Like a cherry, a seven and lemons
The words that come to mind
Are no match.

Another hit from his cigarette
His pile of literary coins diminishes
He takes another swallow of booze.

Jackpot!

Triple sevens
The pen comes alive
Phrases of rhyme flow over the pages

Simultaneously
The pen hits the desk as the ice clinks in the empty glass
He extinguishes his Pall Mall.

Surfs up

There is no complicated formula;
I have no magic pen.
Only inspiration and imagination dictate;
With what words my poems begin.

I have no way of knowing;
How the next line will progress.
I do not carefully calculate;
Which words I will use next.

The flow comes from within;
From my soul and through my heart.
Which defines the very difference;
That sets my work apart.

Unlike the ordinary poet;
Who possesses a shallow mind.
I have visions of what I cannot see;
Much like a man who is blind.

I go where the feelings take me;
And let my subconscience be my guide.
Clinging to my pad and pen;
I sit back and enjoy the ride.

Words are tossed out of my head;
Like passengers from a capsized boat.
Only when the literary waters calm;
Do I go back and read what I have wrote.

I can relate very well to this next poem, as I have spent most of my adult life volunteering in different organizations and on several committees.

I am a former member of the Mt. Zion Lions Club. I served on the Liquor Commission for them as well as the Village of Mt. Zion.

I also served on the Planning & Zoning Commission for the village. Currently I am serving as Union President for USW Local 193g, formally serving as a Steward and on the IRC Committee.

I have announced the Mt. Zion High School varsity football games for the last 20 years, also track meets, mud drag races, mud volleyball and 10k runs during that time.

I coach J.F.L. Football for 23 years as well several seasons coaching baseball, wrestling and boys & girls basketball.

I have both sympathy and admiration for those willing to subject themselves to the sometimes aggravation of serving others.

This poem was written after my wife came home from a band booster meeting in which some of those who hadn't helped out all year, decided to show up and bitch about how someone else did something.

Volunteering is like voting. If you didn't bother to do either one, then shut the hell up when things don't go your way.

The Boosters

We are known by enough people;
We couldn't get away with having an affair.
But we're not famous enough;
That anyone would care.

Noone is asking for autographs;
There are no paparazzi around.
But we are a familiar face;
When we walk through the town.

We are just average Joes;
We are just average Janes.
A lot of people recognize us;
They just don't remember our names.

We are the volunteers and citizens;
On advisory committees and boards.
The chairs and coordinators;
That everyone looks toward.

To get the job done;
Make the event go off without a hitch.
We are the last to take credit;
And they are the first to bitch.

So get off you duffs and volunteer;
And give us a helping hand.
We are not in it for ourselves;
We are just supporting our band.

One thing about being active socially is the connections you make with other people.

The next 11 poems were written for other people, some of them friends and some of them family members. Each one of them having a special meaning in my life.

Emotions In Bloom

She keeps her feelings hidden;
Showing emotion only behind locked doors.
Her silence forever present;
Except when a teardrop hits the floor.

Avoiding conflict and confrontation;
Withdrawn and timid to a fault.
As the baby of the family;
Becomes the youngest adult.

Deaths of loved ones and family tragedies;
Have forced her into her cocoon.
But have faith my lonely child;
Like a beautiful flower, soon you too will bloom.

You will grow to be open and vibrant;
Your beauty and color will shine so bright.
The others in the garden of life;
Will be amazed at your resolve and might.

You are the centerpiece of the bouquet;
In this old gardener's eye.
Remember to make a flower grow;
Rain has to fall down from the sky.

Be not afraid to open up;
Spread your joy and your tears.
You will take root and you will grow;
Become strong and conquer your fears.

Mystery Writer

She stands alone at the bar;
Seemingly in her own world.
There is something hauntingly familiar;
About this hat wearing mysterious girl.

She hasn't spoken a word;
But her message is loud and clear.
She has a story to tell;
One I would like to hear.

The attraction is a spiritual one;
Not physical in nature.
I don't want to know her name or number;
I only want to know what motivates her.

We strike up a conversation;
I ask about her true passion.
She says she wants to write children's books;
Now I understand the attraction.

She desires to be a writer;
And I am an author and poet.
I told her I knew she had a story;
That I would really like to know it.

We shared our thoughts on writing;
Our influences and inspirations.
I told her about my poetry books;
As she told me her aspirations.

I gave her some tips on publishing;
Thanked her for taking the time to chat.
Next time I run into her;
I want to hear the story behind the hat.

Moonbeam Memories

It's the middle of the morning;
About a quarter past three.
I'm sitting on the front porch;
Watching the moon jump the trees.

I'm carrying on a conversation;
Though it's mostly in my head.
Did you know you can still talk to people;
Even though they are dead?

I'm talking to three loved ones;
That I lost this spring.
I still can hear their voices;
Though they're not saying anything.

I tell them what I am thinking;
I tell them how I feel.
The way the stars twinkle when I ask a question;
It all seems so surreal.

The next time you have a problem;
Or are struggling to understand life.
Try talking to those who have gone before you;
In the middle of the night.

It will calm your soul;
And comfort your mind.
Surfing on the moon across the sky;
That must be one hell of a ride.

I hope I get as lucky;
As Kenny, Bev & Jim.
If I ever get those angel wings;
And St. Peter lets me in.

Our Loss

Today I received the tragic news;
Of the death of my friend Greg Drum.
Not only a friend but a classmate;
Of Mt. Zion High School, "Class of '81".

Today we mourn one of our own;
Our hearts are heavy with sorrow.
The memories he made in yesteryear;
Will enable us to get through tomorrow.

His spirit, his smile and zest for life;
The example he has left us to follow.
Will allow us to savor each moment with him;
Though his passing is a bitter pill to swallow.

Live this moment to the fullest;
And cherish our time we spent in the past.
Not only have we lost our friend;
The group from '81 has lost some class.

Remembering Richie

The last few years of his life;
His mind and body rankled with pain.
On a bitter cold January night;
Those demons went up in flames.

A tragic event no doubt;
To his family and his friends.
But, his painful life is over;
His eternal life now begins.

Peacefully he rests;
In the mansion God built for him.
He sits at the right hand of the Father;
With Pete, Katie, Maggie & Jim.

Once again he walks without stumbling;
His mind is quick and sure.
Safe in the arms of God;
His pain is nevermore.

Our lives have all been touched;
By his kindness and gentle love.
Our loss is lessened in knowing;
He rests in peace in heaven above.

Hayward Barnes

The song by Allen Jackson;
Talks about a small town southern man.
Unless you have actually met one;
You would not fully understand.

I had the privilege of knowing one;
By the name of Hayward Barnes.
He lived along the Elm River;
Born and raised on that family farm.

A friend to all that knew him;
With a kind and gentle soul.
One of the few that I can say;
Who truly had a heart of gold.

To make sure you felt at home;
He would completely go out of his way.
He'd share with you his knowledge;
Or just listen to what you had to say.

He shared his land and home with me;
And treated me like I was kin.
I'm truly blessed and honored;
To call Hayward Barnes my friend.

Thank you for the time you spent;
Teaching me how to be a good man.
How my farm feels like home to others;
When I'm willing to share my land.

I know how fortunate we are;
To have what we do.
A lesson that I learned;
Taught to me by you.

Final Closing Time

The neon signs are all silent;
All the beer taps have run dry.
The jukebox has been turned off;
There is no more fish to fry.

Nothing but empty bar stools;
Lined up neatly in a row.
No ballgame on the television;
Idle dice with noone to throw.

I finish the last bottle of whiskey;
One last toast I hold up high.
In honor of Elmer Sherman;
It is time to say goodbye.

All the tabs have been zeroed out;
The cash register has an empty till.
That last shot is hard to swallow;
Much like a bitter pill.

Your liquor license has expired;
Time to join Pee Wee, Dixie & Katie.
I turn the lights out and stare into the darkness;
As I lock the door and throw away the key.

Alley Of The Dolls

My Mother is quite a woman;
But she'd never be what she is.
If it wasn't for the guidance;
Of Maggie, her big sis.

She taught her how to be a woman;
A Mother and a Wife.
Mom is not the only one;
That Maggie effected their life.

She's been the patriarch of the family;
Since Grandma Katie has been gone.
She's been an inspiration for all of us;
And her memory will live on.

The Cardinals were her team;
Bowling was her passion.
There is not a bowler in this town;
Who hasn't benefited from her actions.

So next time you see the lightning;
And feel the thunder as it hits.
That's just Maggie, Katie & Lucille;
Picking up their splits.

Dear Mother I Thank You

I learned so many lessons;
Not found in any book.
Some strongly suggested, some gently offered;
All I willingly took.

You taught me how to be a Daughter;
To be a great Mother and a good Wife.
Molded me and led by example;
Yet, you let me live my own life.

How to deal with adversity;
Prepared me for this very minute.
You knew there would come a time in my life;
Where you would no longer be in it.

Gone may be you physical presence;
But your memories and lessons live on.
I am the person I am;
All because of my Mom.

So dear Mother I thank you;
For all that you have done.
I can only hope someday my halo shines as bright as yours;
In the eyes of my two sons.

Lonely Hunter

What is it going to be like?
When I have to make that drive.
Down to the empty farm;
When you are no longer alive.

How will I survive it?
When you are no longer here.
The thought of hunting alone;
Never before gave me this much fear.

Will I be able to handle it?
When I pull that truck into town.
Will I reminisce and smile;
Or will I break down?

When I down the big buck;
Or that 25 lb. boss Tom.
Will I be able to rejoice;
Or will that feeling be gone?

I hope I never have to face;
That fateful moment or day.
But if it happens to come;
Give me the strength to stay.

Because that is our passion;
My huntin' buddy and I share.
And I know "in spirit";
You will always be there.

And if I go before you;
Don't give it up because I'm gone.
In order to begin the healing;
The hunt must go on

Patriotic Brother

I've covered the bodies of fallen soldiers;
Flown high over the cemeteries in France.
Was proudly displayed on the Enola Gay;
The day we dropped the bombs on Japan.

Watched over the troops in Korea;
And on Iwo Jima on top of the hill.
Above the jungles in Vietnam;
I fly for the M.I.A.'s that remain there still.

I have waved in the Middle East;
Where ever the U.S. troops reside.
On front porches in every town's main street;
Displayed with respect and pride.

I am the American Flag;
The red, the white and the blue.
Two-hundred plus years of service;
I fly proudly because of people like you.

I wrote this next poem for the 200th anniversary of the birth of Edgar Allen Poe. I actually submitted it to be read at the official ceremony in Baltimore, Md., to commemorate the event.

I received a nice letter from the Communications Director, Baltimore Office of Promotions & The Arts, saying they were forwarding it to the Baltimore Area Convention & Visitors Association which was organizing the event.

So if you were in Baltimore for the celebration, you may have seen or heard the poem at some point.

Most poetry lovers know the story of the yearly visitor to the grave of Edgar Allen Poe on the anniversary of his birth. Only this time on one of the biggest birthdays ever, the visitor was a no show.

I hope I didn't jinx the occasion.

Return Of The Raven

A familiar flutter interrupts a quiet night;
Moonlight shines off the ebony wings.
He lands upon the weathered stone;
As the Angel of Death begins to sing.

The yearly ritual takes place;
On a cold dark Baltimore night.
He returns to the cemetery;
To honor the Master of Fright.

A half drank bottle of Cognac;
And a rose times three.
The admirer who placed it there;
Remains unknown to thee.

As the midnight bell tolls;
He returns to his safe haven.
Another tribute has been completed;
With the return of the raven.

The original 'Prince of Darkness';
May once again rest in peace.
At least until the next flight;
Of the demon-eyed coal black beast.

The legend continues to live on;
The mystery grows even deeper.
In memory of Edgar Allen Poe;
Every poets' Grim Reaper.

One thing my poems will always do is freeze a moment in time like a photograph. The old saying "A picture is worth a thousand words", is true.

However, sometimes words are needed to accurately describe the true picture of what you see.

Mammas Are Just Like Jesus

The bible says we should not have false idols;
That is what we are taught when we are young.
But we all have a hero other than Jesus;
A hero that goes through life unsung.

They protect us with the same vigor;
And their unconditional love in which we trust.
To insure we are safe from harm;
They would die for us if they must.

They forgive our sins and shortcomings;
Accept us in spite of our flaws.
But their birthdays are rarely big celebrations;
Without fanfare and Santa Claus.

Mammas are just like Jesus;
Only we crucify them every day;
They die inside because of our actions;
And the way that we misbehave.

You won't find nail holes in her hands and feet;
But you will find forgiveness and open arms.
Jesus may be the son of God;
But he also had a Mom.

Gazing Grandpa

Words cannot describe the moment;
I first held you in my arms.
Stunned by the pure amazement;
I was totally captivated by your charm.

You were just a few hours old;
But your impact was already felt.
As I cradled you to my chest;
My heart began to melt.

I struggled to hold back the tears;
So that I would not cry.
I wanted nothing to cloud my vision;
As I gazed into your eyes.

My actions must seem to many;
As being a little odd.
Layla Mahlon you had me mesmerized.
You truly are a gift from God.

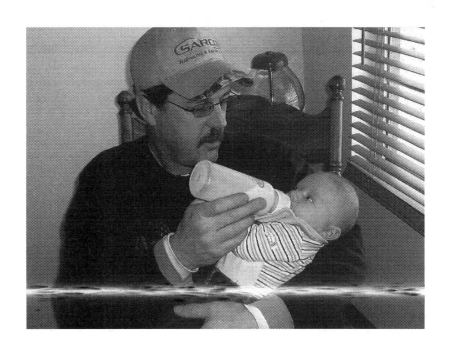

Be Proud

When I look at what you have become;
I am amazed at what I see.
The way you have matured into a man;
And what you have come to be.

There was a time I questioned myself;
The tough love I threw your way.
Whether right or wrong, you must admit;
It helped you become who you are today.

With everything that has happened between us;
And all that we have been through.
Being proud to call me your Father;
Is really all up to you.

I'm not searching for an answer;
Regardless of the outcome.
I just want you to know I love you;
And I'm proud to call you my Son.

Soon you will be a Husband;
Perhaps even a Father some day.
Use me as an example, good or bad;
To avoid the mistakes I made.

God's blessings on your marriage;
I wish you the best of luck my Son.
I pray that when you look into the mirror;
You are as proud as I, of what you have become.

Colors On My Heart

To some it is just a picture;
For others it is useless ink.
But before you criticize my decision;
Take a moment to stop and think.

I lost my daily contact with them;
Which led to more separation in time.
Maybe I'm being delusional;
Or perhaps I'm being blind.

It's my way to keep their faces before me;
In front of the memories I've lost.
Although it doesn't lessen the heartache;
Or the price those years lost have cost.

It cannot replace the interaction;
Of all the missed smiles and tears.
But now I have them with me every day;
And we'll be together for years.

Understand my decision or not;
You haven't gone what I went through.
Think about that before you criticize;
My actions or my tattoo.

Senior Night

They say you're not my kin;
Because you don't have my DNA.
But I don't give a damn how they feel;
Or what they have to say.

I wiped your butt when you were little;
Cleaned up vomit when you were ill.
They say that doesn't prove anything;
To this day they deny it still.

They say you're not my child;
Only a Step-Daughter at best.
But who gave you your first driving lesson at the farm?
To help you pass that test.

They say we're only related;
Because your Mom and I are married.
But who towed your car out of that snowy field;
The day you got it buried.

Though I'm not down on the field;
But looking down from up above.
I'm like an angel in the sky;
Sending down my love.

Though you don't have my blood;
I'm the only Dad you have known.
I think that gives me the right;
To call you one of my own.

By now I hope my absence;
Is fully understood.
I'm in the booth for a very good reason;
To announce to the world my Daughter, Susie Underwood.

I Did My Best

It really does not matter;
That our DNA is not the same.
It's not even an issue to me;
That they don't have my last name.

You will have to forgive me;
If it looks like I'm being selfish.
But they are just as much my girls;
As they are anyone else's.

Whether a shoulder to cry on;
Or just someone to talk to.
It's a responsibility I took on;
And one I lived up to.

I didn't turn my back;
On the two children that I have
I just expanded my role;
As a Father and a Dad.

I did the best I could;
To spread my love around.
Despite all I have done;
There are those who put me down.

There is plenty of love in my heart;
For all four of my kids.
I just did what I had to do;
And my best is what I did.

I'll be the first to admit that my life hasn't turned out the way I envisioned it as I was growing up. It has had very few moments of calm and serenity.

But, last April I was blessed with collectively the greatest week of my life, where everything was perfect. My mind was clear, my worries were non-existent. It was like being on the greatest drug in the world without any side effects.

I don't know if I will ever have another week or even a day on earth that will ever duplicate that time. But, if the days in heaven are anywhere near as wonderful as that week was, I'm ready to go.

Seven Perfect Days

It is always a sad day;
When the season comes to an end.
You find yourself all alone;
After a week of being with friends.

The laughter has all died;
Guns and decoys are stored away.
But the pictures in the photo album;
Remind us of those wonderful days.

Some days we had success;
Failure was never seen.
Even when the only turkeys we saw;
Were the gobblers in our dreams.

Hot dogs cooked on the campfire;
Taste better than a steak from the finest chef.
Even with the taste of deepwoods off cologne;
Mixed with my beer and tobacco breath.

In all my forty-six years;
Never a finer week have I ever had.
Than the seven days I just spent;
Hanging out with my buddy Gregg and Dad.

One of my biggest problems is accepting the constant changes in life.

To me the kids are no longer kids. They are an extension of what they were.

The parents, grand parents, aunts & uncles have either passed or are a shell of who they used to be.

In my mind I am the same as I always was. But, when I look in the mirror, I see that I am not.

My youth is gone and over with, much like the pages of my books that have already been read. My future is yet to be seen.

But quick enough will be revealed like the final pages of this book.

Soon there will be nothing left, save for the pictures and words that describe what was my life.

Allowed To Fly

To some it is just a multi-colored cloth;
To others a red, white & blue rag.
But it takes more than just simple thread;
To keep those stars and stripes intact.

It takes veterans from every branch;
To protect her from defeat.
Their bravery displayed and their blood shed;
To insure freedom for you and me.

With very little thanks from us;
They continue to soldier on.
The air, land and sea are secure;
Their duty forever goes on.

She has stood the test of time;
Forever may she continue to wave.
Thanks to those in uniform;
We are still the home of the brave.

So take time to display her proud;
Remember why she is allowed to fly.
And thank the ones who were willing;
To risk their lives and fight for you and I.

Nature's Art Show

As the summer sun begins to fade;
And autumn is on the brink.
I watch the kaleidoscope of colors;
It's a poet's time to think.

I watch the grass turn to brown;
My tanned skin as it turns ashen.
The blue skies slightly blend to grey;
Nature's scenes, worthy of an artist's passion.

My eyes see an unframed painting;
Created by an unseen hand.
A real live panoramic mural;
That cannot be duplicated by man.

Michelangelo, Picasso or Warhol;
None of them had the range.
To create a more beautiful image;
Than watching the seasons change.

1984 Is Here

Big Brother is definitely watching;
Just like George Orwell predicted.
"The Man" is sitting in a director's chair;
Watching our lives like they are scripted.

He knows how much water is in our bath;
And who we call on the phone.
Through a satellite millions of miles away;
He's viewing color pictures on our homes.

Our account balance is known to the penny;
What we just purchased at the store.
Skeletons in our closets are exposed;
Privacy is never more.

We are like human stars;
Floating across the sky.
Big Brother is an astrologist;
And tracks us with his watchful eyes.

So plot your next move very carefully;
You are under the microscope lens.
God is not the only one watching;
Or keeping track of your sins.

Don't believe me, do something stupid;
It will be recorded for all eternity.
But alas there is one glimmer of hope;
Maybe someone will steal your identity.

A Second Chance To Dance

I skipped my senior year homecoming;
Because I was dating a girl from another school.
At 17, something that seemed so right;
At 46, you realize you were a fool.

These were my last days with my classmates;
And I let them pass right by.
The memories that I'll never have;
They will carry with them for life.

I cannot make up for that night;
We will never have that last dance.
But I promised I would not repeat that mistake;
If I ever got another chance.

Reunions, I've been to them all;
I never pass on the street without saying hello.
When I got the call to meet them for drinks;
There wasn't any way I was going to say no.

We talked about the good times and old days;
Went through the yearbook to jog our memory.
Shared some wine, cheese and spirits;
In the basement of the winery.

Thanks for giving me a call;
And taking the time to ask me to come by.
If I don't see you before then;
I'll see you at the next reunion, of the Class of '81.

Monuments And Memories

I watched them pour the footings today;
For my Mother and Father's gravestone.
I delivered family heirlooms to my son;
Including one of my original written poems.

It has been quite a reality check;
As I sit on the porch and reminisce about the past.
I sit here feeling both euphoria and sadness;
Thinking, "What if this day was my last?"

Would they know that I loved them?
Would they have realized I did care?
Or would they think I had abandoned them;
Because of the times I wasn't there?

What happened to all those years;
That are suddenly now behind me?
How did I catch up to the future:
That is now walking right along beside me?

It won't be too much longer;
Until I will be living on borrowed time.
And there will be graveyard workers;
Pouring the gravestone of mine.

I have more things to give away to my daughters
So there will be more days like this.
I just hope I live long enough;
To be remembered by my grandkids.

Seasons Of Emotional Change

Like a summer day that lasts forever;
His mood is light and carefree.
Unaware of the winds of change;
That will blow in from the northeast.

His mood falls like the autumn leaves;
Slowly and lifeless he drifts.
Till motionless, idle and pale;
Totally engulfed in the winters grips.

Struggling to remain whole and intact;
Surrounded by darkness and cold.
Like a curling leaf on the ground;
He clings to whatever he can hold.

Friends pop up to surround him;
Like an acorn cradled in the spring grass.
He firmly digs into life's soil;
Not looking back at the seasons past.

Rejuvenated by the warmth of protection;
His mood rises high like the summer's sun.
Surviving the cycle as does the acorn;
As his new life has begun.

Time

On your first date as a teenager;
Time goes by so fast.
But not nearly as quick;
As your teenage years of the past.

When you are young you anticipate;
Hoping the future will quickly come.
Then in your golden years;
You recollect and reflect on past fun.

While during the workday;
Time seems to stand still.
It ticks away too rapidly when rushing;
To a loved one who is deathly ill.

Time is a precious commodity;
Of that there is no doubt.
Spend your allotted time wisely;
Before your time runs out.

Live each moment to the fullest;
Cherish every minute the same.
Unlike sports, in this life;
There is no overtime in this game.

Satan's Mistress

With eyes as black as cobalt;
That pulls you in just like a spell.
A body as beautiful as heaven;
With a mind as wicked as hell.

Don't let the innocent smile fool you;
Or girlish curls that frame her face.
She'll sneak up on you like a summer storm;
With the same furry and feverish pace.

She will pull you into her arms;
And hold you tightly in her grips.
You cannot escape the temptation;
Even when you taste the poison from her lips.

Her tongue cuts like a dagger;
And burns much like a flame.
You have now become a victim;
Of the dark angel with no name.

Smitten by the Mistress of Darkness;
Deceived by the pretense of trust.
You've been captivated and succumbed;
Killed by temptation and lust.

Only while laying on your deathbed;
As you breathe in your last breath.
Will you finally come to realize;
You have been kissed by the angel of death.

Free America

They have taken God out of our schools;
And replaced him with silence.
The peaceful suburbs and neighborhoods;
Are full of crack houses and violence.

They're trying to take away my protection;
Quell my opinions and free speech.
It seems the American dream;
Is no longer in reach.

Prisoners, terrorists and illegal aliens;
Now somehow have all the rights.
American citizens are now suppressed;
Not allowed to speak out or to fight.

The hammer and the sickle;
Will soon replace the stars & stripes.
That beacon of hope is slowly fading;
As they extinguish lady liberty's lights.

It is time for the people to take back America;
Make her the promise land she once was.
Weed out the gutless leaders and politicians;
America's future is up to us.

Whenever I get in one of "my moods", my wife always asks me, "What's wrong?" I always have the same answer.

"The demons are dancing."

When we first got together she didn't understand what I meant by that. She would try to pry deeper, which only makes the demons laugh and more brutal to deal with.

She now knows when she hears those words, my mind is being tortured by thoughts and images that she cannot even begin to understand. So she no longer tries to understand them. She leaves me to my own devices to deal with them.

They can't be subdued with alcohol and pills. Believe me, I've tried. Through my poetry I have discovered who I really am, what I can control and what I cannot.

Some of these last ten poems are pretty intense and personal. But finally I can say with certainty, **"The demons are done dancing."**

Literary Sweaters

The night is full of mist;
From a steady falling rain.
The kind of just right night;
That stimulates a poet's brain.

Cool air surrounds my body;
As a chill caresses my face.
To a poet it is the same feeling;
Ordinary people get from a lovers embrace.

Held tight in the arms of loneliness;
There is no better time.
To crochet a literary sweater;
Or stitch together words of rhyme.

An outfit only a few can wear;
A style not fit for all.
An original piece not mass produced;
Available only from the writer's mall.

It's quite a little store;
That I've opened in my mind.
Racks full of literary sweaters;
Each original and one of a kind.

Unknown Visitor

An image over my shoulder;
A faint vision does appear.
I turn to take a look;
But no one is there.

Sometimes the figure is dark;
Sometimes it is sort of aglow.
Who is this mysterious figure;
Is it someone that I know?

Why does it vanish;
When I turn to see?
If it doesn't want to be seen;
Why is it following me?

Is it a guardian angel;
Protecting and keeping me well?
Is it the Grim Reaper or a demon;
Coming to take me to hell?

Sometimes I live in fear;
Sometimes I live in serenity;
My life will be in turmoil;
Until they reveal their identity.

Prophetic Dreams

Awakened by haunting dreams;
That always seem to come true.
Why is it that my wishes;
Never come to fruit?

Thoughts I can control;
Seem to get lost in the night.
Replaced by omens and signs;
When I close my eyes too tight.

I toss and turn with apprehension;
I go to sleep in fear.
Afraid I will see tragedy;
Or a loved one will appear.

The message is not always clear;
The clues are sometimes intertwined.
I struggle to find the answers;
Before I run out of time.

I don't expect you to understand;
My rationale or what I've said.
But when I lay down to sleep tonight;
Please stay out of my head.

Broken Down

My hands are worn and callused;
There's crows feet around my eyes.
My joints feel like the ninety years old;
Although I am only forty-five.

Life has run my through the wringer;
And raked me over the coals.
I've had my share of injuries;
Surgeries and broken bones.

My mind is starting to fade;
And definitely reached its peak.
My strength and stamina diminished;
As my muscles have become weak.

I was once as nimble as a cat;
Full of energy and drive.
But I crammed a lot of living in a short time;
And used up all my nine lives.

Like a once classic car;
That is ready to pile on the junk heap.
I'm glad I'm not a dog;
Because they'd probably put me to sleep.

Burnt

The fires have been lit;
Ignited by the Goddess of Evil.
My soul singed by the flickering flames;
Have left me burnt by life and feeble.

I walk through glowing embers;
Being fanned by the demands of others.
Trapped in a ring of blinding light;
As thick smoke begins to smother.

Choking the life out of me;
The very air that I breathe.
The searing heat stinging my corneas;
My eyes can no longer see.

The screams of the damned are piercing;
My ears begin to bleed.
My flesh and bone turns to ashes;
Until nothing is left of me.

Cremated by the ungrateful and self-righteous;
Cast into the flaming grave.
With no remorse, respect or consideration;
For the love to them I gave.

Silent Night

Sometimes my thoughts are random;
Most times they are well thought out.
At times the voices I hear, whisper;
Usually they scream and shout.

Silent and private conversations;
That become public when I write.
Usually dormant in the daylight hours;
They run rampant in the night.

No way to mute or silence them;
There is no volume control.
Immune from my attempts to suppress them;
They feed upon my soul.

Playing games with my thoughts;
Like a rag doll, my brain gets tossed around.
The voices will never be silent;
Until they lay me in the ground.

They say there is no rest for the wicked;
My mind must be evil to the core.
I wish for that silent night;
When the voices are nevermore.

Wasted Crucifixion

I deserve to die on the cross;
Not because I am a savior.
I deserve the nails and thorns;
Because I am the failure.

God sacrificed his only son;
To pay for my sin.
It is not his fault;
He didn't deserve that end.

My body is the one;
That should be hanging there in shame.
He should not be the one;
To shoulder all the blame.

I am the imperfect sinner;
He is not the one who should have died.
I am the only one;
Who deserves to be crucified.

Redemption

I cannot right the wrongs I've done;
No matter how I might try.
Thinking about the pain that I've caused others;
Makes me want to cry.

I've shunned those who needed help;
Told those who cared to go away.
Stood fast with my decisions;
Always refusing to be swayed.

I don't know why I am like this;
Only that is the way I am.
I know I'll end up lonely and alone;
But I just don't give a damn.

Distancing myself from other people;
To protect my heart from pain.
But hurting others to save myself;
To you must seem insane.

To me it is proactive;
For some day I will be gone.
Maybe that day you will hurt no more;
And that day I will right my wrong.

Freedom Writer

I've never been one to apologize;
For anything I have done.
No matter whether right or wrong;
I always stick to my guns.

I say what's on my mind;
What I say is what I meant.
I know people have been hurt;
But that wasn't my intent.

I must live by my principles;
And pay what price I may.
I refuse to shut my mouth;
Or have you censor what I can say.

The pen is mightier than the sword;
As the age old saying goes.
May my pen never be idle;
And my ink well never closed.

Lest you not judge my opinions;
Instead dissect my logic and reason.
When did freedom of speech become a crime;
And standing up for your beliefs become treason?

I have literally struggled for days trying to figure out how to wrap this book up. I guess all I can really say is I hope you have enjoyed all four books of my poetry collection, **'A Look Into My Soul', 'Dark Eyes; Deep Mind', 'Beyond The Smile' & 'The Demons Are Done Dancing'.**

"Thank you for accompanying me on this journey, for if I had to walk this path alone, I could never have completed the trip".

Danny Mahlon Underwood

Last Performance

Should they list the accomplishments;
And the accolades of my life?
Should they include the pitfalls;
The struggles, the failures and strife?

It is a complicated picture;
The life that I have led.
Should they include my favorite saying;
Or the last words that I said?

A visitation with a viewing;
Or a candlelight memorial?
I say just call the mortician;
And get on with the burial.

There is no need for a service;
Or to put me on display.
Drop me in the ground;
And go on with your day.

Don't put your life on hold;
When I am no longer around.
Just take a moment alone;
And listen to "Tears of a Clown."

Listen to the lyrics;
Hear the pain as Smokey sings.
You want to honor my wishes?
Just do this one little thing.

No doubt it will be tough;
For you to listen to this song.
But the circus is over for me;
It's time for this clown to move on